AF488453

Hello DETROIT

BY JEANETTE PIERCE

ILLUSTRATED BY DAVE TOENNIES

LAKE SUPERIOR
CANADA
MICHIGAN
WISCONSIN
Lake Michigan
USA
Lake Huron
ONTARIO
DETROIT
ILLINOIS
LAKE ERIE

HELLO DETROIT!
WE LOVE YOU!
YOU HAVE WONDERFUL PLACES, OLD AND NEW!

1

HELLO DETROIT, WITH YOUR BEAUTIFUL BUILDINGS!

HELLO RENAISSANCE CENTER, TALLEST OF THEM ALL!

HELLO PENOBSCOT TOWER AND YOUR GIANT RED BALL!

HELLO DETROIT, WITH YOUR 300 PARKS!
HELLO BALDUCK, WITH YOUR GIANT SLEDDING HILL!

HELLO ROUGE PARK, WITH
YOUR TWO POOLS TO FILL!

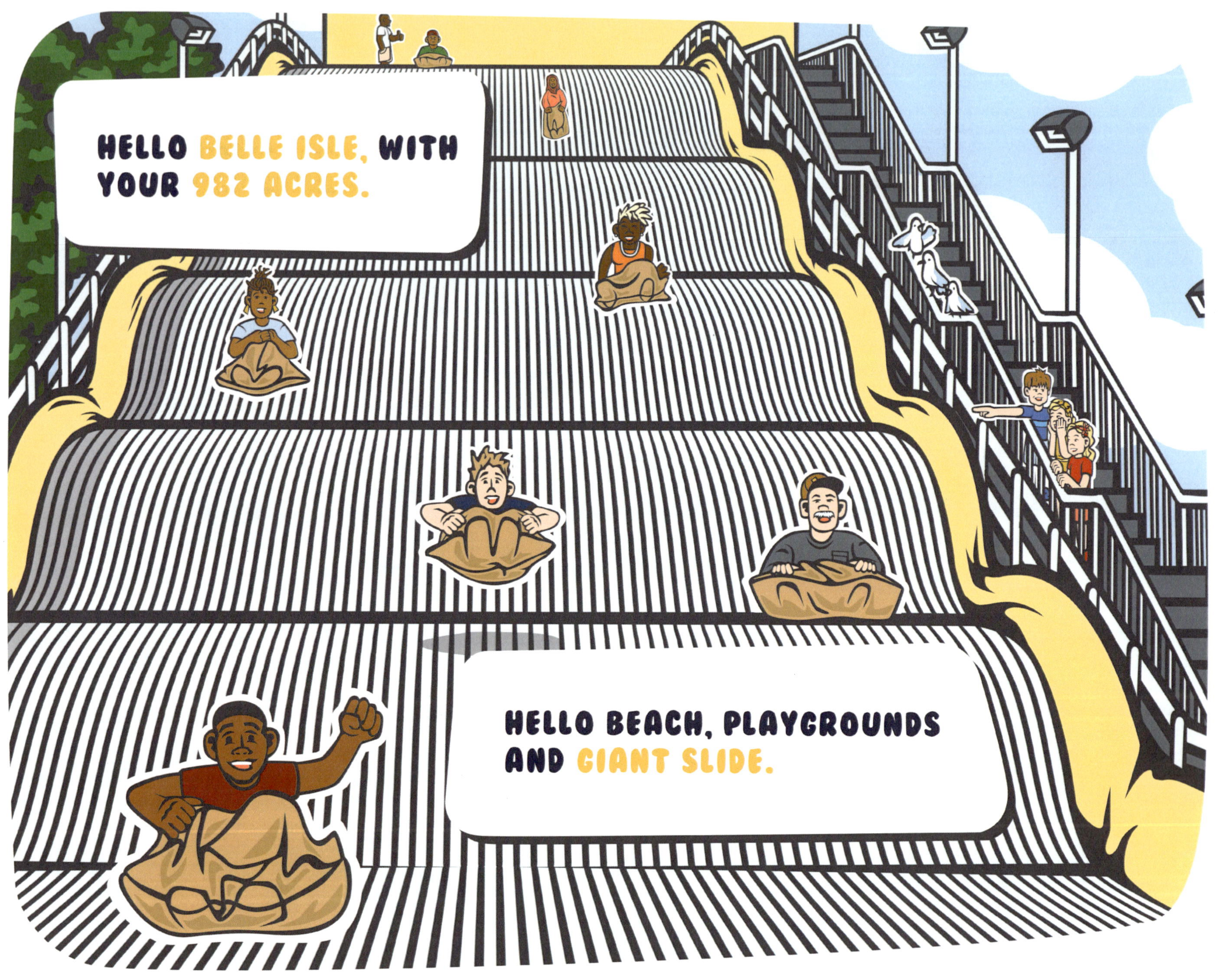

HELLO BELLE ISLE, WITH YOUR 982 ACRES.
HELLO BEACH, PLAYGROUNDS AND GIANT SLIDE.

AQUARIUM
HELLO DOSSIN, AQUARIUM AND CONSERVATORY FOR HAVING FUN INSIDE.
DOSSIN GREAT LAKES MUSEUM
PERRY'S VICTORY
LAKE ERIE

HELLO RIVERWALK, WITH YOUR INTERNATIONAL VIEW!
WINDSOR, ON

HELLO CAROUSEL, BUTTERFLY GARDEN AND SPLASH PAD TOO!

HELLO EASTERN MARKET SINCE 1891!
EASTERN MARKET
313
2 FOR 1
LOOK!
SAVE!
SHOP SMALL

HELLO VEGETABLES, FRUIT AND MURALS THAT MAKE VISITING SO MUCH FUN!
WATERMELON
YOYODA

HELLO ART PROJECTS GALORE!

HELLO HEIDELBERG, ARTIST VILLAGE, DABLS AND SO MANY MORE!

HELLO DETROIT LIBRARIES, BIG AND SMALL!

HELLO PROGRAMS, BOOKS AND WELCOMING SPACE FOR ALL!
MOBILE LIBRARY
DETROIT PUBLIC LIBRARY
DETROIT PUBLIC LIBRARY

HELLO WORLD-CLASS MUSEUMS THAT OFFER SO MUCH TO SEE AND DO!
HELLO MUSEUM OF AFRICAN AMERICAN HISTORY AND DIA TOO!
THE DETROIT INSTITUTE OF ARTS
CHARLES H. WRIGHT MUSEUM

HELLO SCIENCE CENTER AND HISTORICAL MUSEUM TO NAME JUST A FEW.
MICHIGAN
Science
CENTER
DETROIT HISTORICAL MUSEUM
MODEL
DETROIT HISTORICAL MUSEUM

DALLY IN THE ALLEY
LAGER HOUSE
Baker's
WORLDS OLDEST JAZZ CLUB
SINCE 1934
DETROIT TECHNO CITY MOVEMENT
MAY
CASS CORRIDOR
N.C.C.U.
FOX
Hitsville U.S.A.
BERRY GORDY
MOTOWN MUSEUM
CLIFF BELLS
Saint Andrew's
J-DILLA
MOTOWN
FOX
ks Finest Entertainment
HELLO DETROIT MUSIC THAT'S MADE THE WORLD DANCE THROUGH THE YEARS.
HELLO MOTOWN AND TECHNO THAT DETROIT PIONEERED.
THE FILLMORE
BIG SEAN | ROYCE DA 5'9"
DANNY BROWN

THE WHITE STRIPES
ARETHA FRANKLIN
AMPHITHEATRE
JAZZ FEST
MUSIC HALL
HELLO JAZZ, GOSPEL, ROCK, AND HIP HOP THAT DETROITERS LOVE TO HEAR.
Raven Lounge
& Restaurant
Raven LOUNGE & RESTAURANT
Raven LOUNGE & RESTAURANT ENTERTAINMENT • FRI-SAT. SUN.
LIQUOR BEER WINE
Dine Dan
UNITED SOUND SYSTEMS
RECORDING STUDIO
TON YES

WEST side
EAST side
SOUTH WEST
HELLO DETROIT, YOUR PEOPLE ARE THE BEST! EASTSIDE, WESTSIDE AND SOUTHWEST!

HELLO DETROIT, YOU'RE ALL ABOUT COMMUNITY!
THAT'S WHY YOU'RE AN AMAZING CITY!

THANK YOU TO **THE RIVERFRONT CONSERVANCY** FOR PLANTING THE SEED TO WRITE THIS BOOK BACK IN 2011, WHEN THEY ASKED ME TO BE A GUEST READER AT THEIR WONDERFUL READING AND RHYTHM ON THE RIVERFRONT PROGRAM.

THANK YOU TO **MY TEAM** AT **CITY INSTITUTE** FOR HOLDING DOWN THE FORT AND LEADING TOURS, SO I COULD HAVE SOME TIME TO GET THIS PROJECT TO THE FINISH LINE.

THANK YOU TO THE INCREDIBLY TALENTED **DAVE TOENNIES** OF **TON YES DESIGN**, WHOSE VIBRANT AND DETAILED ILLUSTRATIONS BROUGHT MY WORDS TO LIFE.

THANK YOU TO **HEIDI SCHULTZ**, WHO HAS KNOWN ME SINCE BEFORE I WAS BORN, AND WHO ALSO KNOWS HOW TO EDIT BOOKS.

THANK YOU TO **MY PARENTS, JOHN AND KRISTINE**, FOR INSTILLING IN ME A LOVE OF READING AND A LOVE FOR DETROIT FROM AN EARLY AGE.

THANK YOU TO **MY HUSBAND, RICHARD**, WHO IS SO INCREDIBLY SUPPORTIVE, REGARDLESS OF HOW FAR-FETCHED THE IDEAS MIGHT SEEM AT THE TIME.

THANK YOU TO **MY WONDERFUL KIDS, MARINA, GIA, AND GUS**, AKA **THE CITY TRIPLETS**, FOR INSPIRING ME TO SHARE THE STORY OF DETROIT FROM A CHILD S POINT OF VIEW, AND FOR THE HOURS UPON HOURS OF ROCKING THEM TO SLEEP, WHICH GAVE ME AMPLE TIME TO IMAGINE ALL THE IDEAS FOR THE STORY.

FINALLY, THANK YOU TO **DETROIT**—THE CITY WHERE I WAS BORN AND RAISED, FOR **THE AMAZING PEOPLE, PLACES, AND PROJECTS** HERE THAT MAKE IT MY FAVORITE CITY IN THE WORLD, AND FOR BEING BIG ENOUGH TO MATTER IN THE WORLD, YET SMALL ENOUGH WHERE EACH OF US CAN MATTER IN IT.

THANK YOUS!